First edition © 2024. All rights reserve...

No part of this publication may be reproduced, distributed or transmitted in any form or by any means, including photocopying, recording, or other electronic or mechanical methods, without the prior written permission of the authors, except in the case of brief quotations which must then be accompanied by a reference to the authors of this book.

Lead author

Andreas Trautner

Co-author

Lasse Damgaard Hasselstrøm

Key contributor

Anneline Kirkegaard

Editor

Timothy Young

Reviewer

Chris Kolborg

Table of Contents

Forewords 1
1   Introduction 9
    1.1   Why do so many projects fail? 10
    1.2   A key question 11
    1.3   A powerful, systemic error 13
    1.4   A new paradigm and unifying model 15
2   A powerful, systemic error 17
    2.1   Consequences of the project triangle mindset 18
    2.2   So, what is a project? 23
        2.2.1   What is project success, and how do we define failure? 27
    2.3   The full picture 29
        2.3.1   Part 1: A project is an investment 29
        2.3.2   Part 2: An investment – in change 33
    2.4   The eight project parameters 35
    2.5   Project triangle-focus vs Investment-focus 37
    2.6   "Something we simply need to do" 44
    2.7   Two essential definitions 47
3   People-focus 49
    3.1   Machine-mindset 52
    3.2   System 1 vs System 2 61
        3.2.1   Overcoming System 1 decision making 63
4   Change in an organizational context 69

4.1	Why have a strategy?	71
4.2	The three integrated elements in an organization	71
4.3	What is a change portfolio?	73
4.4	Everything can be changed	74
5	A new model for understanding projects	77
5.1	Important implications of the Project Investment Chain	80
5.2	Uncertainties and pitfalls	82
5.3	The stakeholders and the psychological contract	86
6	Conclusions	89
6.1	A short and simple truth about projects	91
6.2	The Project Investment Chain® by DIS/CREADIS	94
6.3	We already have what it takes	95
7	Perspectivation	99
7.1	Discovering what was hidden	99
7.2	A note on sustainability	102
7.3	Concluding words	103

FOREWORDS

Mastering project management is like becoming a skilled chef. At the beginning, we follow tested "recipes" established frameworks that offer us the essentials of planning, budgeting, and risk management. Much like a novice cook that measures ingredients and follows each step in the recipe, many project managers adhere to these frameworks with the intent of delivering projects on time, within scope, and according to expectations.

But true mastery, in both cooking and project management, is about moving beyond these basic steps and adding capabilities which are based on mindset and skills.

A project, as this book reveals, is not merely about meeting a specific budget or a deadline; it is an investment in change. Like a chef who learns to experiment with flavors and techniques, adjusting each dish to suit the tastes of those at the table, a skilled project manager adapts to the unique needs of stakeholders and the evolving landscape of the project. The "project triangle" of time, cost, and scope is merely about the deliverable; true success requires a broader view that considers the benefits, costs, risks, and the people change for each change initiative.

Our book, Project Reset, offers a fresh approach to project management, guiding readers toward an investment and people-focused mindset that balances rigor with flexibility and control with creativity.

This book serves to help you learn not just to deliver following a "recipe" but to orchestrate successful outcomes, crafted thoughtfully for each unique project.

We strive towards - and invite others to strive towards - leading and delivering projects that, like a well-prepared dish, are both impactful and deeply satisfying to those they serve.

Kenneth S. Jensen
CEO, DIS/CREADIS

As CTOO and Project Owner at Lyras, I recognize the crucial role effective project management plays in maintaining our high standards and meeting the growing expectations of our customers and stakeholders. In our industry, projects are more than just a means to an end they form the backbone of our growth and innovation. Mastering project management is essential for us to deliver the CO_2 reductions, water savings, and increased resource efficiency that our customers require.

The path to becoming a truly great project manager often lies in hands-on experience, much like an apprenticeship in a skilled craft. As with many craftsman trades, project management requires a deep understanding of nuances, unspoken expectations, and the art of navigating challenges that are not found in textbooks.

Over the years, we have enjoyed a rewarding collaboration with DIS/CREADIS and Andreas T, benefiting from their vital expertise and many inspiring reflections on the project management craft. So, when I learned of DIS/CREADIS and Andreas' desire to share their accumulated insights more broadly through this book, I was delighted.

This book addresses those aspects that typically take years to learn. It articulates the hidden skills and insights in a clear, accessible way, making it a powerful tool for both new and experienced project managers. It is essential reading for anyone looking to improve or update their project management skills and provides basic knowledge in "Project Fundamentals" as well as crucial insights into "The Project Invest-ment Chain".

These concepts are not just theoretical—they represent the practical framework required to ensure that every project aligns with our strategic goals, stakeholder expectations, meets deadlines, and stays within budget. Mastering these elements can make the difference between project success and fail-ure. For those seeking to elevate their project management skills and drive their projects to success, this book offers a unique opportunity to learn from the best practices and avoid common pitfalls.

I highly recommend it as a valuable resource in your journey towards mastering the art of project management.

Nete Zarp Nielsen
CTOO, Lyras A/S

In today's rapidly evolving world, the concept of Communities of Practice (CoP) has become increasingly significant. As we navigate through complex challenges and strive for continuous improvement, the power of collective learning and shared expertise cannot be overstated.

I have been working with thought leadership through my role as leading The Global Engineering at CREADIS for the past four years. Our core tool for building knowledge is our CoPs, and the "Project Reset" is a powerful outcome of the CoP of project management.

CoPs are groups of individuals who share a common interest, passion, or profession. They come together to share knowledge, solve problems, and innovate. These communities are not just about networking; they are about creating a space where members can learn from each other, collaborate on projects, and develop new skills.

Our organization has embraced the concept of Communities of Practice to foster a culture of continuous learning and innovation. By encouraging our employees to take part in these communities, we enhance their professional development and drive the organization's growth and success in a structured manner.

This book delves into the best practices of project management, highlighting the importance of structured methodologies and frameworks to overcome traditional challenges. It emphasizes the need for clear definitions of project success and failure, as well as the importance of aligning project objectives with organizational goals.

The guiding lighthouses are a key to the success of a CoP. They are experienced and knowledgeable members who guide and lead the communities and share their insights and perspectives. Through regular interactions, they enable the exchange of best practices, the discussion of challenges, and the exploration of new ideas among the members. This collaborative approach fosters innovation and improvement within the field of project management. This book is a powerful product of the project management community, showcasing the best practices and frameworks that have emerged from the community's collective wisdom.

It is truly inspiring to witness the clarity that emerges when highly skilled individuals come together, share their curiosity, and strive to make an impact in their field. I extend my thanks to Andreas Trautner and Lasse Hasselstrøm for their exceptional leadership in this area.

'Project Reset' is a shining example of the magic that can happen when such talented individuals collaborate.

Magnus B. Erlang
Senior VP, Global Engineering &
Competence Center, DIS/CREADIS

As an associate professor and researcher in the field of project management, I have encountered numerous methodologies and frameworks aimed at refining project success. It is notable that many of these approaches focus on traditional metrics such as time, budget, and scope, often encapsulated by the well-known "project triangle." While these factors are undeniably important, they do not capture the full complexity of what it means to manage a project successfully.

"Project Reset" takes a refreshing departure from these conventional views, with the authors advocating for a shift towards understanding projects as investments in change. This perspective represents a profound rethinking of how we define project success and manage project outcomes.

One of the book's key contributions is its emphasis on the purpose of projects. In a field where the completion of deliverables is often mistaken for success, "Project Reset" reminds us that the real measure of a project's success lies in its ability to bring about meaningful change. This change is the essence of the project's purpose, and it must remain the central focus, from project initiation through to closure and beyond.

The authors also highlight an often-overlooked aspect of project management: the importance of the deployment phase. While much of the literature centers on project closure, "Project Reset" extends the perspective by focusing on whether the promised change materializes post-project closure. By shifting attention from the completion of the project triangle to the realization of benefits, this book advocates for a more comprehensive and meaningful approach to project management.

"Project Reset" contributes to the literature by promoting a more purpose-driven approach to projects. It argues that the true success of a project cannot be fully understood at the moment of closure but must be assessed in the longer term, as the project's intended change is realized and integrated into the organization.

Maja Due Kadenic
Associate Professor, MSc, PhD
Dept. of Business Development & Technology
Aarhus University

Trautner & Hasselstrøm

1 INTRODUCTION

Humans have been conducting projects for thousands of years. While our ancestors may very well have applied structured management methods, any semblance of this has long since been lost to history and thus cannot be relied upon for inspiration; as such, the tools, methods, and methodologies people and organizations currently use to manage projects are relatively new.

As with our ancient forbears, everything started with *tools*. In 1910, Henry Gantt introduced the Gantt chart, which provided practitioners with a brand-new way to visualize projects. CPM and PERT methods followed in 1958, but we will move past these and argue that the modern project management era began in the early 1970s, when project managers began devising new practices specifically created to overcome common reasons for IT project failure. In 1996, these practices were codified as the PRINCE2® and the PMBOK®, in this book referred to as "best practice project management", because they were designed to tackle not only challenges in IT-projects but common, well-known reasons for project failure. This involves various elements such as crafting project feasibility studies, engaging closely with key stakeholders, learning from experience, setting up the project's governance, agreeing on project objectives and planning how to deliver on them, managing problems and uncertainties, and following project progress on the plan, and the status of the project parameters.

A year earlier, in 1995, another popular method—Scrum—was presented in a research paper. Its development had been initiated in the early 1990s, and its strategy focused on team-level projects and the rapid development and testing of IT deliverables.

In 1995, Rick Maurer published *Beyond the Wall of Resistance* and in 1996, John Kotter published *Leading Change*. In these books, which are well-known as major works within the field of change management, the authors discussed why it is often difficult for organizations and people to change the way they do things and how to get it right.

Since then, practitioners have put forth numerous project management methodologies, frameworks, methods, and tools not to mention a myriad of books and papers published by academia all with the goal of helping organizations reach higher levels of project execution success.

1.1 Why do so many projects fail?

Over the years, many organizations have attempted to improve their project management culture by implementing new PM methodologies, methods, and tools. Some have gone through several within short periods of time.

However, when organizations try to become better at running change initiatives, most will fail to achieve any significant, measurable improvements in the success rate of their projects. Also, as we will explore later, many projects concerning product change (e.g., product development projects) also fail or struggle.

Consequently, the reality is that most projects in organizations fail[1]. The organizational landscape is littered with struggling, failing, and failed change initiatives, often referred to as projects, programs, changes, transformations, must-win-battles, and strategic initiatives, and moreover: the PM frameworks, methodologies, methods, and tools do not seem to be working.

One of the consequences hereof is that the challenges that organizations faced with their projects 10 years ago are the same that they have today, and will still have tomorrow, and 20 years from now – unless we start doing something differently.

1.2 A key question

The key question, therefore, is:

What exactly is it that people and organizations need to do differently to become better at running projects?

Our years of expertise including our involvement in countless projects, reviewing many others, and hundreds of hours spent interviewing professionals (e.g., project managers, program managers, project board

---

[1] PRINCE2®7. 2023. *Managing successful projects.*

members, team managers, tech leads, project team members, and line managers) and training thousands of people in project, program, and portfolio management has lifted the veil on several shared aspects of failed projects that are key to understanding what is going on, hereunder:

- projects struggle and fail due to the very same problems that best practice project management was developed to cope with decades ago
- overall, people generally lack the skills needed to constructively apply best practice project management
- when an organization tries to become better at managing projects, the common "solution" is to follow the same path: People jump the gun and begin designing and deploying new governance structures and ceremonies to comply with; new generic stage/gate models and checklists for people to follow, new process-models to adhere to, templates or artefacts to fill out, applying IT-tools but clearly, such impatience has done nothing to solve the problem.

The persistence of these problems over several decades suggests one or several powerful, systemic errors root causes which cripple organizations' attempts to improve their project culture by making it exceedingly difficult for people to apply proper best practice project management, thereby effectively coping with these well-known reasons for project failure.

1.3 A powerful, systemic error

Training thousands of people in project management has rewarded us with unique insight into the existence of a notable project management blunder:

People find it daunting to define what a project is.

Think of the story of the three blind men examining an elephant one examines its ear and thinks the elephant is a fan; the next feels its leg describing it as a tree; and the third, feeling its trunk, describes the elephant as resembling a large snake.

The competing camps of project management are no different—the only thing they indisputably agree upon is the fact that they are discussing a project. Furthermore, each framework and methodology boast their *own* project definitions—with different schools of academia developing their own as well. These varied definitions are by no means variations of the identical understandings of each facet of project management; so, it is no surprise that confusion abounds!

Even if the definitions that we are referring to here are vastly different, they can be grouped into two overarching categories:

1) *Category #1* defines a project as something that delivers an output (or product) per specific deadline and budget.
2) *Category #2* defines a project as something that not only delivers an output (or product), but also a result that is favorable when considering the resources and effort required to achieve it.

These two categories ultimately express two separate, tangential ways of defining:

- What a project is
- When a project is successful
- When a project has failed

Consequently, they represent two fundamentally divergent ways of thinking or paradigms within the science of project management and, therefore, each view defines success differently.

As we hinted earlier, most people approach a project as something to be delivered per predefined deadline and budget: this is how most projects are launched and managed, with success measured accordingly. Unfortunately, this reality reflects a titanic misunderstanding, which can easily lead to capsizing projects.

1.4 A new paradigm and unifying model

As with all science, the role of project management science is to provide paradigms and models primed to help people address and overcome related challenges and issues, and to help provide answers to the fundamental questions within the area. If the paradigm within a science cannot provide the necessary explanations, it is in crisis[2] and must be replaced.

Our primary concern when authoring this book is to fully address the question: Are there any indications suggesting the science of project management is currently in crisis? The answer, unfortunately, is a resounding YES. First and foremost, in the world of projects, most have continued to fail for common and foreseeable reasons not only in the distant past, but over recent decades. Secondly, the science of project management has failed to agree upon the most basic definitions; people still argue about what a project is, what project success is, what project failure is, and what project management is.

In this book, we present a new, unifying model poised to inform and streamline the science of project management: providing crystal-clear definitions that lay a solid foundation for developing bold hypotheses that both practitioners and academia can put to the test for falsification—or corroboration. In doing so, we position ourselves to

---

[2] Thomas S Kuhn. 1962. *The Structure of Scientific Revolutions*.

further develop the field of project management science to ultimately tackle diverse problems in business environs that call for successful change across a wide spectrum of challenges.

Moreover, the new model combines five project management silos deliverable management, project management, change management, benefits management, and strategy execution into one single model. As we demonstrate on the pages herein, these all reflect different perspectives of the same domain.

Zooming out, digesting the contents of this book will arm you with thorough knowledge and comprehension about what a project and project management is (and is not!), as well as the definitions of project success and failure: basic fundamentals we see people struggle with on a daily basis, making it difficult for them to communicate and pull hard in the same direction as they strive to achieve their project objectives and the organization's strategic goals.

2 A POWERFUL, SYSTEMIC ERROR

Over the years, we have been involved in numerous projects across a wide range of business areas, trained thousands of people in project management and related fields including portfolio-, risk-, benefits-, program- and quality management, held countless workshops, reviewed stacks of CV's and interviewed a plethora of Project Managers, Team Managers, Tech Leads, Project Board Members and other project professionals.

What has become clear to us is that most projects are started and managed as *something which must be delivered within a budget and by a deadline.* This is the predominant paradigm, or pattern of thinking, in projects; the mindset that drives people's actions and decisions throughout most projects.

This mindset is illustrated by the popular "iron triangle," which is also referred to as "the project triangle", the "iron triangle", the "golden triangle" or "the magic triangle" (fig. 2.1). This mindset results in people focusing mainly on four parameters: Cost, time, quality, and scope, where quality describes the required features and functionalities, and the scope describes the composition of the "package" to be delivered; that is, what is included and what is excluded.

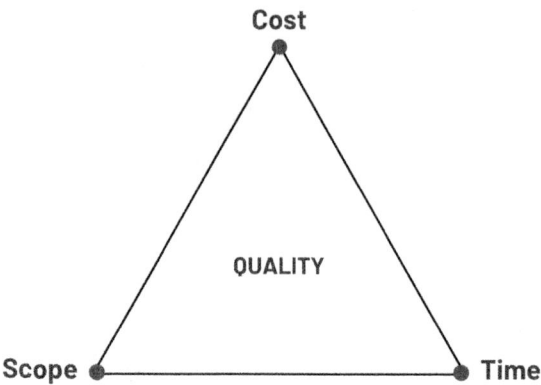

Fig. 2.1. The "Project Triangle".

The triangle is highly popular and widely used for teaching people project management, for example, at Business Schools. According to the International Association of Project Managers (IAPM), "... *the Magic Triangle identifies the interdependencies between the three main objectives of a project: time, cost and quality.*"

However, these are not the sole primary objectives of a project. It is a misunderstanding and starting and running a project with this pattern of thinking, or mindset, often comes with serious, negative consequences.

2.1 Consequences of the project triangle mindset

Mindsets become visible through people's actions, and we can clearly see that whenever the Project Triangle mindset is predominant, there is a strong focus on time and cost and therefore, on starting the project quickly. Consequently, people spend insufficient time studying and establishing clear agreements about the feasibility and attractiveness of the project, the known uncertainties and obstacles, the required quality and scope to be delivered, and clarification of the project in general. Consequently, when the project triangle mindset dominates projects, they typically suffer from a range of problems:

- "Scope creep," where the scope of the project expands slowly or rapidly with little or no control
- The required scope, features and functionalities of the outputs are unclear and not agreed-upon
- Unclear responsibilities of the people involved
- Poor planning
- Lack of proper quality planning and quality control
- The key element of "people change" is poorly managed
- People ignoring huge, foreseeable risks
- Negative consequences of the project are ignored, and positive consequences are overstated
- Lack of control of the project's progress and status
- People lack a mutual understanding of the consequences and/or desired results of the project
- As the project progresses, there is a lot of noise and stress in the project

Recognize any of these problems? If you are a skilled craftsman or woman of best practice project management, you will recognize that these problems are transparent and foreseeable in a project, and can be dealt with relatively easily and effectively by applying the following fundamental elements of best practice project management:

- Finding, discussing, and agreeing on the project's *actual* Business Case
- Applying quality management, hereunder quality planning, and quality control
- Giving the project's stakeholders clear project roles and responsibilities
- Focused, detailed planning.
- Applying best practice risk management
- Managing issues, hereunder management of request for changes and problems
- Closely monitoring the progress and status of the project
- Collaborating and communicating with the stakeholders

It is not a coincidence that the fundamental elements of project management are highly effective for dealing with common, well-known problems. This is by design: project management has been developed over five decades specifically to deal with these obstacles, and these elements are the very backbone of best practice project management.

Unfortunately, whenever the Project Triangle mindset is predominant, people display exceptionally low ability to purposefully apply the fundamental elements of project management. They may, with the best intentions, try to be compliant with the organization's generic project governance set-up, but people will go through the activities and motions of best practice project management with little skill. This often leads to *"project management in name only"* and *"project management in templates only,"* two common examples of where people believe they are conducting project management but perform ineffective ceremonies instead.

Due to the shortcomings resulting from the Project Triangle mindset, decision-makers start thousands of projects, even when they lack fundamental, best practice project management elements, such as:

- A proper and agreed-upon Business Case
- A proper plan, focused on quality planning.
- A defined and agreed-upon scope.
- Proper risk- and issue management
- Strong project organization
- Agreements on how to control real progress and status.

Furthermore, and we cannot stress this enough, in projects where the focus is to deliver something within a pre-defined deadline and a budget, the project is headed by people who want deliverables, and people who believe that they can deliver. In effect, the Project Board therefore consists of only one role: the Senior Supplier. This means that neither the customers and users, nor the investors are adequately represented in the decisions. People may hold the title of Project Owner, or Senior User, but they cannot shoulder the responsibilities of representing these key stakeholders, as the focus is predominantly on delivering something within a deadline and budget.

What is painstakingly clear is that in projects where the project triangle mindset dominates, those involved display a lack of mindfulness and prudence, and they therefore tend to be over-optimistic when starting projects.

As stated by the late, great Daniel Kahneman:
"If there is something that you really want to do, then you are probably overly optimistic about it. Optimism is the source of everything that is good, but it is also the source of a great many failures."[3]

---

[3] Kahneman, Daniel. Jan 13, 2015. *Speech to the World Economic Forum: How to improve decision making.*

The project triangle mindset is a powerful, systemic error that makes it exceedingly difficult for people to effectively apply the elements of project management and make good decisions, as they are focused on a fast or super-fast project start. The reason is that each of the fundamental elements of best practice project management requires patterns of thinking that are entirely different from the project triangle mindset. These patterns of thinking, or mindsets, are rooted in the logical truth of what a project is.

2.2 So, what is a project?

As discussed, the predominant mindset people display when they start and manage projects is the project triangle mindset. However, there exists many definitions of what a project is because there are countless books, manuals, and papers on project management, both within academia and the area of practical project management. Of course, all too often the authors present their own views and opinion of what a project is.

It is not within the scope of this book to conduct a review of every project definition that exists but here are three often-cited project definitions:

- According to the Project Management Institute, *"a project is a temporary endeavor undertaken to create a unique product, service, or result[4]."*
- In the PRINCE2®7 manual, a project is defined as *"a temporary organization that is created for the purpose of delivering one or more business products according to an agreed business case."*
- Turner sees a project as *"an endeavor in which human, material and financial resources are organized in a novel way, to undertake a unique scope of work, of given specification, within the constraints of cost and time, so as to achieve beneficial change defined by quantitative and qualitative objectives[5]."*

The definitions are very different, not only in their wording but also in the mindsets that they convey. This is a huge problem that is not merely about semantics. When there is not one commonly accepted definition of what a project is, there is not one commonly accepted definition of

- What is project management?
- What is the role of a Project Manager?
- What is the role of a Project Owner?

---

[4] www.pmi.org
[5] Turner, J. Rodney. 1993. *The Handbook of Project-based Management: Improving the Processes for achieving Strategic Objectives*. London; McGraw-Hill

- What is project success?
- What is project failure?

If project management is to move forward as a science, then all of us in the field must agree upon the most basic aspects of what a project is. In the immortal words of Socrates (470 – 399 B.C.), "The beginning of wisdom is the definition of terms." This means that if you cannot define a term, you cannot understand its importance and therefore, you cannot conceptualize it.

The key to starting and running successful projects consistently is to understand what a project is, and to apply this understanding as a pattern of thinking, a mindset for applying project management.

This is where we should start:

A project is an investment in change

These seven words capture the essence and irrefutable, logical truth of projects. The statement seems exceedingly simple, yet few people think of projects as investments. However, this is a fundamental characteristic of all projects and the starting point of understanding projects and project management.

A project is clearly an investment where something is invested to bring about a change to stakeholders. What is invested can be energy, funds, time, skills, and natural resources. However, it is essential to understand that other assets are often invested as well. For example, when we at DIS/CREADIS start a project to create a solution for a customer, the decision-makers invest our most important assets in the project:

- The company's brand and reputation
- The relationship with our client
- The relationship with our suppliers
- The project team's well-being
- The owners, or shareholders, funds

The same important assets are invested when people in a public organization start a project to develop a needed change or upgrade, such as a new IT system. In this case, the real investors are the taxpayers.

Clearly, there is much more to a project than just delivering something within the budget and the deadline. It is exceedingly important to understand that there is nothing that anyone can do to change the inherent and true logic of a project. That is what it is and what it will always be. The consequences of failing or succeeding with a project will invariably reflect this truth.

2.2.1 What is project success, and how do we define failure?

How many projects are successful investments in change? It is difficult to say because very few stakeholder project evaluations focus on evaluating the project as an investment in change.

A common approach to assessing how many projects is successful is to simply ask people about their opinion. Scott Keller and Carolin Aiken reported that *"McKinsey & Company recently surveyed 1546 business executives from around the world, asking them if they consider their change programs "completely/mostly" successful: only 30 percent agreed."*

Unfortunately, this practice makes it impossible to know what criteria people are using for evaluating the success of the project, and it is therefore difficult to know what may have gone wrong, and virtually impossible to know if people are correct.

Projects are also often evaluated based on the project triangle parameters. For example, the Standish Group has been surveying projects in the software development industry and have released their findings in the Chaos Report. In 2015, 50,000 software development projects around the world were studied. The Standish Group classifies projects into three categories[6]:

---

[6] The Standish Group. *The 2015 Chaos Report.*

- *Project success: The project is completed on-time and on-budget, with all features and functions as initially specified.*
- *Project challenged: The project is completed and operational, but over-budget, over the time estimate, and offers fewer features and functions than originally specified.*
- *Project impaired: The project is cancelled at some point during the development cycle.*

However, these criteria are flawed. It is *not* possible to evaluate a project on the Project Triangle's four parameters of time, cost, scope, and quality, because it goes against the true logic of what a project is. No matter why people choose to start a project, regardless of what they want out of it, they are investing in change.

Instead, based on the true logic of what a project is:

- *To be successful, a project must deliver the required change AND be a sound investment.*
- *A project has failed if it is not a sound investment in change.*

It should be clear that completing the project on-time and on-budget, with all features and functions as initially specified, does not qualify the project as being a successful investment. To truly evaluate whether a project has been successful or not, we must examine the full picture as given by its inherent and logical truth.

2.3 The full picture

A project cannot be effectively managed by considering the 3 or 4 parameters laid out by the Project Triangle, because there are often more important parameters to consider and manage. These parameters or performance targets are established by the inherent logic of what a project is.

2.3.1 Part 1: A project is an investment

The knowledge that a project is an investment provides us with valuable information because all investments share five fundamental characteristics:

- They are expected to deliver some kind of return on investment, or **benefits**.
- There are uncertainties i.e., **risks.**
- There may be **downsides** to consider, i.e., negative consequences.
- They all involve **costs** i.e., input of some kind of assets (money, people, time, etc.).
- All investments have a **time horizon** i.e., how long will the assets be invested, how long will it take before the benefits can be realized, and how long will we harvest the benefits? Furthermore, when should we start investing, and when should it be stopped?

Consequently, all investments have five parameters, or performance targets, which must be considered:

- Benefits
- Costs
- Downsides
- Time horizon
- Risks

It is incredibly important to note that benefits encompass more than just money. They concern the effect of the positive consequences of the project as an investment on the project's stakeholders. Therefore, we need to consider elements e.g.,

- The organization's brand and reputation
- The customer relationship
- The relationships with suppliers
- The project team's well-being
- The owner's funds and input of other resources

Furthermore, there may be other positive consequences of the project to consider, like achieving certain strategic goals.

Consequently, to judge whether the project is successful or not, every designated positive consequence must be assessed and weighed against the potentially negative factors of the project like costs, downsides, and threats delivered to the organization. Then, and only then, will we know whether the project was a sound investment.

2.3.1.1 A Project's Investment Case

The Investment Case, or Business Case as it is known to most people, is a vital element of project management, and arguably the most misunderstood. Here, we shall clarify the most important aspects of the Investment Case.

Note, this is not a how-to guide of how to make an Investment Case, but vital information needed to understand the full picture.

All investments in change or projects will have consequences for the stakeholders. These consequences can be grouped under the project's performance targets of benefits, costs, downsides, time horizon and risks. This is often called a Business Case. However, the term is unfortunate because it implies that it is about "business," which makes people think about money. Instead, we suggest using the term "Investment Case." A project's Investment Case is a description of the investment in change, and it should describe both the positive and negative consequences of the investment, and not necessarily in monetary terms. Many projects, e.g., in the public sector, are not delivering benefits in terms of money, but e.g., as better service to the citizens.

Because every project will have consequences for its stakeholders, each individual project has an Investment Case. These consequences will reveal themselves eventually. Some may be desirable; others may be highly undesirable. All investments in change should have their true Investment Case revealed and agreed to by the stakeholders, particularly the decision-makers. The purpose of a project's Investment Case is to provide the stakeholders with a clear overview of all the project's consequences, positive as well as negative, so that they can determine whether the project is an attractive and desirable investment in change, or whether it may be better not to start the project.

Therefore, an Investment Case must offer at least two options: invest in the project, or not. As such, the Investment Case is a foundation for decision-making. This should continue during the project to continuously show if the project is still a sound investment or not – just as you would do with all other investments. After the project, the Investment Case will be used to ascertain whether it was actually a promising idea to start the project and will help the stakeholders understand whether there are any consequences that must be managed.

It is paramount to understand that the purpose of an Investment Case is not to coerce the decision-makers into starting a change initiative. Rather, the Investment Case and the project's potential consequences must be discussed and owned by the decision-makers. It is not a description of how brilliant a new idea is. What would be the point?

After all, any change idea can be made to look attractive simply by over-inflating the positive consequences of the change initiative and turning a blind eye to the negative consequences.

The Investment Case is not a filled-out template. Rather, it is an iterative and inclusive process, a tool for dialogue where one or several change ideas are scrutinized with skepticism from an investment perspective and fundamental agreements are outlined across the stakeholder landscape.

Finally, an Investment Case is the only way of describing an investment in change. It is where project management starts and indeed, where portfolio management starts. Without Investment Cases, it is not possible for the senior management to effectively manage and control an organization's portfolio of change investments.

2.3.2 Part 2: An investment – in change

The last part of the definition is also important: A project is an investment – in change. Projects are investments launched with the purpose of delivering change to stakeholders. It can be a quite simple change or an exceedingly complex and difficult change.

Overall, changes can be divided into two main categories: *Product change and people change*.

1) Product change is:

    a. a new product/deliverable/output
    b. a change to a product/deliverable/output
    c. a product/deliverable/output that is discontinued

Product change can be described by its features and functionalities using **scope** and **quality**.

2) People or culture change refers to *"what we do around here."* An organization or individual can either
    a. start doing something
    b. stop doing something
    c. change the way something is done

It is particularly important to understand that product change will not necessarily create the desired change. To achieve the desired change, you need to change the way *"we do things around here"* i.e., the people change.

While not all projects are aimed at delivering people change; for example, from a supplier or sub-supplier's perspective, the people change parameter should always be considered before the project is started to ensure that:

- The project's scope is correct.
- The project delivers what is needed to support the people/cultural change.

- The project delivers the required new ways of working.
- The *real* risk exposure of the project is recognized and owned from the beginning by considering how difficult it will be to achieve people change.
- The project will be a sound investment in change.

We use the performance target *"Aspired New Ways of Working"* to describe the required and envisioned people change.

2.4 The eight project parameters

Now that we have agreed that a project is an investment in change, we can examine eight project parameters that should be managed throughout the life of a project (Fig. 2.2), and which must be considered when evaluating whether the project is successful.

It may be argued that one parameter perhaps deserves closer attention than the others: All parameters are uncertain to a degree because they are forecasted and estimated based upon current data coupled with the practitioner's prior knowledge.

Therefore, there must be a strong focus on uncertainties, or risks, which is a fundamental parameter for all investments, and especially for projects because they involve two major risk areas: Product change and people change.

Fig. 2.2. The eight essential project performance parameters that must be agreed and managed throughout a project.

That a project is an investment in change means that a project must cover three different focus areas:

1) Delivering products as described by scope and quality
2) Delivering people change as described by new ways of working or operating
3) Making the project a sound investment, which requires focus on
    a. Benefits, hereunder strategic goals
    b. Downsides
    c. Costs
    d. The Time Horizon of the project and the investment
    e. Risks - threats, and opportunities

These three focus areas can be seen as three overall categories of risks to a project. If they are ignored, or otherwise poorly managed, the project has an increased risk of failing to be a sound investment in change. Here, it is important to understand and embrace the fact that these risk categories are a part of all projects, whether ignored or dealt with.

Consequently, when deciding if a project should be started or not, these three risk categories must always be considered, discussed, and managed as risks.

2.5 Project triangle-focus vs Investment-focus

When comparing the project triangle to the "Project Sun," it should be clear that four incredibly important project parameters are missing from the project triangle, hereunder:

- Benefits
- Downsides
- Risks
- Aspired new ways of working

To manage the project as an investment in change, people must focus not only on the four parameters of the project triangle, but also on these four additional parameters. When people start and manage projects with a focus on all eight parameters, it is called investment-focus[7].

Ignoring any of the eight parameters will reduce the likelihood that the project will become a sound investment in change. Therefore, a single-minded view of project management concerned only with the project triangle mindset comes with an increased likelihood of project failure, because it promotes a faulty approach, where the focus is not on the benefits, downsides or risks, which are a major part of all investments; nor is it on people change, which is often vital for succeeding with the project.

Consequently, there is an enormous difference between managing a project with the project triangle mindset, or with investment-focus. Starting and running a project with project triangle focus means that easily foreseeable, and therefore manageable, risks are ignored or poorly managed because people are not being truly mindful of the project, so they cannot apply proper project management, which requires investment-focus.

Experience has shown that the main reason projects struggle and fail is because ignored and otherwise poorly managed risks become small problems, which subsequently materialize into big problems, or even

---

[7] Andreas Trautner & Chris Kolborg. 2020. *The Six – why projects fail and how to succeed*

explode into full crisis. This inevitably creates a noisy, stressful, and confusing working environment that may damage the organization's brand, customer relations, the team, while wasting the owner's funds and bringing other downsides to the organization. Consequently, most projects fail because they are set up to fail from the beginning (Project type A, fig. 2.3).

Imagine, for a moment, rolling a snowball down a steep slope covered in fresh snow. At first, it picks up a little bit of new snow and becomes bigger. However, before long, it is out of control, rolling ever faster, picking up more snow and debris, becoming a juggernaut of destruction destined to destroy anything in its path. Such a case almost invariably occurs when risks are ignored at the outset of a project.

Project type B (fig. 2.3) is a typical illustration of a project where people are investment-focused and collaborating, which means that they are focused on exercising due diligence from the very beginning, and on spending time and making an effort to apply proper project management to the project. That often means that the stress level in the project environment is relatively high at the beginning of the project as people are working hard to set the project up to succeed by preemptively addressing foreseeable risks and obstacles.

After a stretch of time, when the project goes into execution mode, the stress-level becomes relatively low, which denotes a calm, safe, energizing project environment. Some minor peaks are likely to occur, e.g., when issues materialize, but they are managed in a calm and controlled manner.

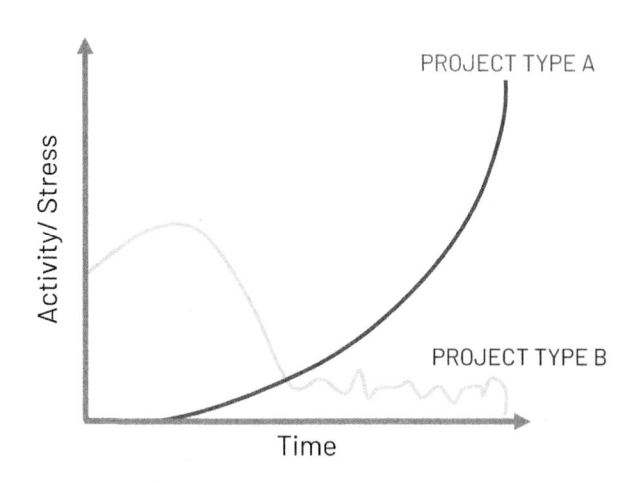

Fig. 2.3. The two typical conceptual activity/stress-curves of projects: The stressful project journey (type A), and the investment-focused and collaborative project journey (type B)

The starting point of each stress pattern communicates a vital story: Proper preparation is paramount to setting up the change initiative to succeed as an investment. To bypass thorough preparation is to accept a high risk that the change initiative will fail to become a good investment. The forceful adage used by the British Army called 7P also applies to project management:

"Proper Planning and Preparation Prevents Piss Poor Performance."

It is straightforward: poor preparation leads to struggling and failing projects because it ignores potential uncertainties. This leads us to a valuable and fundamental insight:

Projects typically do not struggle and fail due to sudden and unforeseeable events beyond the control of the project manager, the teams, and the key stakeholders. Instead, they struggle and fail mainly because readily foreseeable and significant threats to the change initiative are either ignored, accepted, or otherwise poorly managed right from the outset. As these threats materialize into problems and even crises, the focus will shift to firefighting as it gradually becomes impossible to move the project forward.

Thus, in projects where the predominant mindset is the project triangle mindset, people do the wrong things such as starting projects too quickly. They also fail to do the right things because they are not being careful enough and because they do not apply proper project management.

Here are a few key examples:

- A project's Business Case, or Investment Case, is developed to critically scrutinize the project as an investment. It is a feasibility study to answer the question: Should this project really be started? Is this a promising idea? However, when the project triangle mindset is dominant, people simply want to start the project as quickly as possible. Consequently, there is no reason for making an actual, objective, and strong Investment Case. If an Investment Case is made at all, it is only to get permission to start the project.

- The project's organization is set up to ensure that the key stakeholders are represented properly throughout the life of the project. In projects where people are driven by the project triangle mindset, the Project Owner is often very keen to get the project started fast, which is not how it should be. The Project Owner must be the investment owner and exert proper care and caution with the investor's funds. This often leads to situations where the only *real* role present on the decision board is the Sr. Supplier.

- Planning is about rehearsing the project as an investment and dealing with the foreseeable obstacles and pitfalls proactively. As we know, proper planning takes time, and people with the project triangle mindset often do not see the need for this. *"I prefer to plan by myself,"* a Project Manager explained to us, *"... because it is much faster."* This is a clear manifestation of the project triangle mindset, and of the second fundamental mindset that we will discuss in the next chapter.

- Quality management is about ensuring that there are clear agreements about what the project must deliver. Often, the project triangle mindset pushes people to start the project before these agreements can be made and really understood. This often leads to a narrow focus on technical requirements and not on the fundamental customer quality expectations.

- A major facet of risk management is to prevent the project from failing as an investment by managing uncertainties proactively before they become problems or crises. With the project triangle mindset, the focus is not on the projects as an investment and people are not mindful and prudent. Therefore, only a few (or no) risks are identified and managed. Additionally, risks are often identified by the project manager and not by the entire project organization.

- A part of issue management is to manage changes to the project in a controlled fashion. Changes that are not controlled and managed may easily capsize the project due to unforeseen consequences. In projects dominated by the project triangle mindset, people have little or no time to manage issues in a controlled way and end up doing ad hoc management and firefighting.

Consequently, whether people apply investment-focus, or the project triangle mindset will have a profound effect on the key stakeholders' attitude towards decision-making and managing uncertainties and obstacles, and therefore on the investment's risk exposure. The mindset also plays a decisive role in people's ability to apply proper best practice project management to:

1) Delivering products as described by scope and quality
2) Delivering people change as described by new ways of working or operating
3) Making the project a sound investment

Consequently, the mindset that people apply to a project will have an enormous effect on the likelihood of succeeding with the project.

2.6 "Something we simply need to do"

The logical truth of a project is that it is an investment in change. It naturally follows, then, that whenever one or several stakeholders believe that a change is needed and commit resources to achieve a change, it is undeniably an investment in change and, therefore, a project.

This is important because best practice project management has been developed to help people start and run successful investments in change. Therefore, we have tools to address the endeavor of starting, executing and closing down projects. The best practice project management elements can be applied with benefits to any change: The Business Case or Investment Case, planning, risk management, issue management, setting clear goals, measuring progress – the application of these elements should not be restricted to investments in change in organizations. Rather, these are all elements that can and should be applied to many, even most, situations, as implied by many project definitions.

Because people fail to understand that any investment in change is a project, decision-makers start thousands of projects, even when they lack fundamental, best practice project management elements, such as:

- A well-thought-out Business Case
- A proper plan, focused on quality
- A defined and agreed-upon scope
- Proper risk- and issue management
- Strong project organization
- Agreements on how to control real progress and status.

Consequently, many changes are not managed as projects because people are unaware that they are starting a project, i.e., an investment in change. It is important to understand that everything in an organization can be changed. That does not mean that everything *should* be changed, but how can the decision-makers decide what to change, and how to make that change successful? The answer is: By using best practice project management. Unfortunately, this is often not done.

Instead, they approach their desired outcome as if it falls under the vague, amorphous category of *"something we want"* or *"something we simply need to do."* There is a large category of projects that fail because people are not even aware that they are starting a project, i.e., that they are investing in change.

This lack of a strategy tends to occur when people have set their minds on something that they have already firmly concluded is paramount to future success. This can be seen everywhere – not only in organizations, but also in people's private lives, where money is often wasted in pursuit of changes that end up being less important than they seemed at first or end up having too many negative consequences.

According to Daniel Kahneman, *"Nothing in life is as important as you think it is, while you are thinking about it"*[8].

Furthermore, *"If there is something that you really want to do, then you are probably overly optimistic about it. Optimism is the source of everything that is good, but it is also the source of a great many failures."*[9]

The best practice project management elements have been developed to help people critically scrutinize their change ideas, to consider and manage the uncertainties and, if necessary, to set up clear goals and

---

[8] Daniel Kahneman. 2011. *Thinking – fast and slow*
[9] Daniel Kahneman. Jan 13, 2015. *Speech to the World Economic Forum: How to improve decision making*.

plan each phase of the project while monitoring its progress and the status of the investment in change.

2.7 Two essential definitions

We now know that a project is an investment in change. Hereof follows that:

1) a project manager is "an investment in change-manager"
2) project management is" investment in change management"

These two insights and truths are essential for understanding how to run projects, and for understanding the essence of the craftmanship required to be a project manager. A project manager must focus on managing and controlling the benefits, the downsides, the costs, the time, the new ways of working, scope and quality and most importantly: The risks, i.e., the uncertainties that may prevent the project from becoming a sound investment in change. At its core, project management is the craft of reducing the risk of failing with the project by effectively applying the elements of best practice project management.

The implication is that:

Whenever people consider a change, any change at all, they should apply the elements and structures of best practice project management.

It is imperative that we start managing our change ideas with well-known, battle-tested elements of best practice project management. Changes made without these elements often turn out to be poor investments with unforeseen negative consequences, while failing to deliver the expected benefits.

Furthermore, the use of best practice project management elements is not restricted to big projects. Any change, no matter how small it may seem, may benefit from people taking their time to reflect on the change as an investment using project management.

3 PEOPLE-FOCUS

As previously discussed, highly effective projects must be managed with a mindset we call Investment-focus, where the objective is to ensure that the project is a successful investment in change. This mindset is the very foundation for best practice project management, and investment-focus is a fundamental cornerstone.

There is an equally important cornerstone to be mindful of: experience has shown that an additional mindset is vital for running successful projects, and the absence of this mindset increases the likelihood of project failure. We call this mindset "People-focus," and it derives from a fact so obvious that many fail to recognize it:

A project is an investment in change made **by people, for people**

Ignoring this fact is a well-known reason for project failure. The ancient tale of the Tower of Babylon concerns a project to build a tower that would reach to the heavens, the realm of God. God intervened by giving people different languages. Once people could no longer understand one another, the project failed.

People may debate how to interpret the tale, but from a project leadership and management point of view, the story is straightforward: The Tower of Babylon is a project that failed because people could not communicate, and therefore, they could no longer successfully collaborate.

We will argue that this is exactly why so many projects struggle and fail in modern times: People do not communicate well because they do not speak and understand a common language of project management. At its core, a project consists of people collaborating, communicating, and co-creating to achieve a desired result: making the project a sound investment in change.

Getting this done involves five different and integrated areas that must be deftly managed (fig. 3.1). There are two types of change that can be delivered, i.e., product change and people change. Furthermore, the project must deliver benefits and achieve specific, strategic goals. The overall focus is to make the project a sound investment, as defined by the five project variables and performance targets in the project's Investment Case. Not all projects include people change, but most do, and it is of utmost importance that the stakeholders consider the people change element and how to manage it from the project's inception.

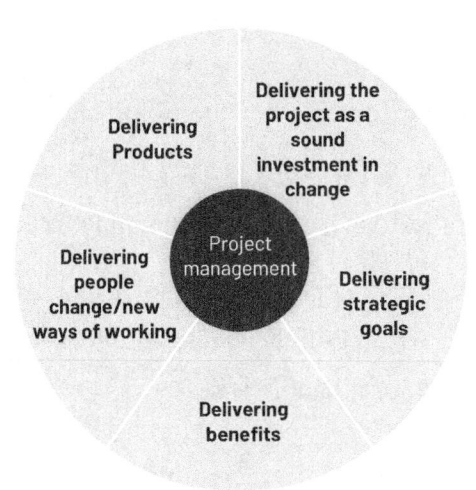

Fig. 3.1. The five overall areas of a project that must be managed.

There are stakeholders within each area as well as throughout the entire project, which means that they have a stake or interest in one, several, or all of the project's performance targets.

To ensure each area's success, the stakeholders must collaborate and co-create to deliver what is required. A precondition for this is that people communicate in an agreed-upon fashion. Without effective communication, it is difficult for people to collaborate and co-create, as emphasized by the ancient tale of the Tower of Babylon.

3.1 Machine-mindset

Unfortunately, People-focus is not the dominant mindset in projects. Instead, people often approach a project with a mindset that is very different from People-focus; a mindset that may be called a "Machine-mindset", because people think of their project's organization as a machine that can be "programmed" and "automated" into operating in a standardized, linear, predictable way.

The Machine-view mindset is incredibly common in the world of project management and can be recognized by its strong focus on rules and procedures, process models, templates, checklists, and IT-tools, all of which are designed to dictate that each phase of the project is completed without variation, according to a predetermined process. In a project-organization with Machine-mindset, *"work is done"* often means that the correct documents have been produced according to an agreed stage/gate model. Consequently, in projects where the Machine-focus is predominant, real project management is often replaced by project administration, where the communication is largely one-way, consisting of people sending internal emails and documents around the organization. There are two strong negatives to this approach—the first is the lack of People-focus, and the second is that the project almost inevitably will have very narrow parameters from the outset, mainly time and costs.

Furthermore, "Machine-focus" can often be clearly seen when organizations are trying to improve their project culture. Because people believe so strongly that everything about a project can be standardized and automated, their focus is typically on:

- Designing processes for people to follow
- Making templates for people to fill out
- Using IT-tools for project management activities like planning and financial reporting
- Designing generic stage/gate models for people to meticulously follow
- Making checklists of tasks to be done and documents to be generated
- Providing people with certificates within project management

Consider this list for a moment. It should be clear that when people and organizations try to improve their project culture, they almost always focus on deliverables and products, hoping that this can somehow create the desired new ways of working. However, as many organizations have learnt the hard way, such activities and documents will not lead to more successful projects. Instead, they will create new ways of working in which people mistake activities for results. This will lead to time-and-money-consuming ceremonies where the focus is on improving the ceremonies and not on improving the project culture

– a rain dance where the main purpose is to improve the dance but not to achieve the objectives.

For some organizations this turns into an ever-spinning cycle, where new processes and tools are implemented, often based on the latest hype in the market. Employees respond with increasing process-fatigue and often leaves them confused about internal best practices.

Like the Project Triangle mindset, the Machine-mindset is very powerful, and it is therefore often difficult for people to understand why templates, process models and tools will not automatically lead to better projects. To explain this, consider the model below (fig. 3.2). It is a graphical representation of how a couple should place their feet when they dance the Tango. However, it must be made clear that the diagram does not show the Tango. It is merely a graphical representation of *one* aspect of the Tango, and we cannot forget that the Tango is a dance that is told through music and movement. A couple that is dancing the Tango expresses emotions like joy, pain, power, trickery, love, heartbreak, loss, yearning, passion, and romance. The diagram shows none of this.

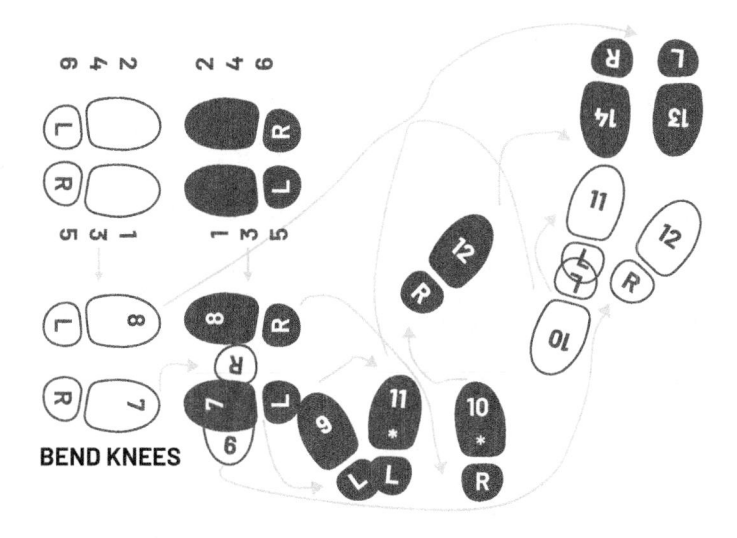

Fig. 3.2. This is not the Tango.

Consequently, the diagram does not relay what dancing the Tango is *actually* about. Even if you manage to place your clumsy feet as illustrated by the diagram, it should remain clear that you will not be dancing the Tango. Even if you had the diagram, the right clothing, shoes, and the right music, you would find yourself unable to dance the Tango without skills or without the "Tango mindset" that you should be expressing.

Hence, within any craft, mindset and skills are imperative. You cannot "program" anyone to become a craftsman or -woman by simply providing them with tools and diagrams, and that is doubly true for project management.

Becoming a true craftsman or -woman in project management takes years of diligent studying, learning, and practicing the elements of best practice project management. Nevertheless, anyone can call themselves "Project Manager" or "Project Board Member" without having studied project management or having any formal training in project management. In Denmark, it takes three years to become a hairdresser; four years if you want to be allowed to cut long hair. In comparison, organizations send people for a 2–3-day training in project management in the belief that such a short training will magically transform them into highly effective project managers. It must be very clear that this *will not* give anyone the skills they need, or the required mindsets.

Instead of focusing on skills and mindsets, organizations focus on producing process-models, templates, IT-tools, stage/gate models, making checklists and setting up ceremonies because these activities can be done relatively quickly and cheaply, and require few, if any, project management skills. Often, organizations use junior employees or student workers for this, which shows the lack of respect, even disdain, for the craft. Producing these deliverables may give people a sense of progress, but these deliverables have a high risk of not creating productive new ways of working.

Paradoxically but predictably, we can see in many organizations that the deliverables that are intended to help the organization improve its project management maturity are being produced and distributed without the application of proper project management. This means that they are not organically implemented into the organization. Therefore, when the organization makes the deliverables "mandatory" to use, it dramatically lessens the chances of full organizational buy-in and will nearly always create an administrative overhead on each project that does not necessarily create any value for the project or the organization.

Therefore, it does not seem that sending people to 2-3-day training sessions in project management increases their skills in managing projects. Instead, people tend to walk away from project management training with only a basic misunderstanding of what project management is, i.e., they walk away with a firm Project Triangle mindset and a clear conviction that project management's sole focus is filling out templates, following a stage/gate model, performing rituals, and sending documents from one level to the next in a strictly-layered "swim lane" project organization (fig. 3.3). This fact is further fueled by the insecurity that lies with many (new) project managers – 2–3-day training sessions will provide some comprehension, but no real skills. Therefore, many people end up with a focus on being compliant with the organization's governance and use this to secure a sense of progress.

In an organization where Machine-focus is predominant, the interaction between people in each of the three swim lanes tends to be very limited, often to only formal meetings centered around documents, standardized templates, or financial reporting, often distributed via emails.

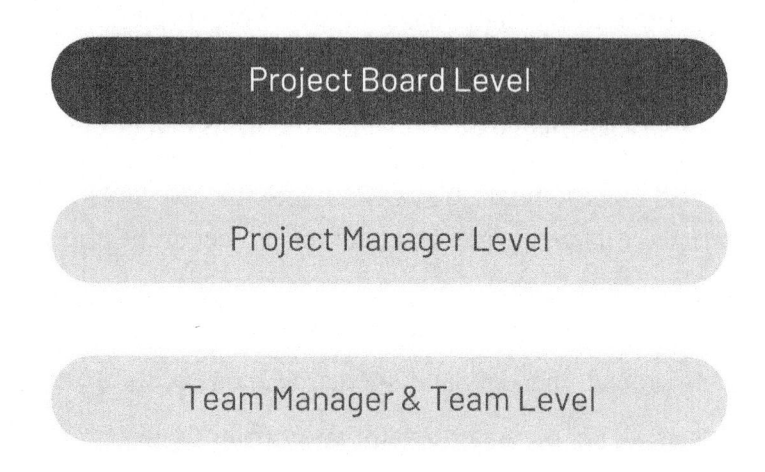

Fig. 3.3. The swim lane project organization often communicates by distributing documents.

The swim lane project organization is based upon a fundamental misunderstanding of project management, and relies heavily on Machine-focus, with a notable lack of People-focus. It is based on the belief that projects are moved forward by sharing documents and performing ceremonies. The question, then, is:

Why is project management so often misunderstood?

The best practice project management methodologies are based on both Investment-focus and People-focus, but it may be argued that these mindsets are implicit and therefore easy to miss. If you view a project through the lens of the project triangle mindset and machine-focus, this is what you will see. Therefore, it becomes easy for the layman to misunderstand what project management really is about.

For example, organizations often want to maintain a set of standardized templates. One of the arguments is that *"the project board members must be able to understand the documents at a glance"* – hence, a focus on efficiency. However, that is a display of Machine-focus. In People-focus, the project board will be deeply involved from the outset in the discussions and the agreements that are later documented, and the format of the documentation becomes much less important.

In a project, all stakeholders or their representatives must collaborate to produce suitable solutions and decisions, and to find a common way to make the project successful. To start a project, to manage it, and come up with the change idea requires people. It includes a range of key stakeholders that must collaborate, co-create and work towards common goals. Therefore, people working on a project must establish a common, shared understanding of the eight project performance targets as well as how to respond to uncertainties and issues, how to communicate, and how to move the project forward towards common goals. A project is people collaborating and co-creating, not a machine that can be programmed by having rules thrust upon the project from the outside.

Consider again the list of common examples of poor project management:

- The project's Business Case is poorly crafted and either misleading, weak, or made to coerce the decision makers into starting the project
- The key stakeholders are not shouldering their project roles and responsibilities
- The quality planning and quality control is done on an ad hoc basis
- The focus is not on the planning, but on putting tasks in a Gantt Chart
- Risks are either poorly managed or ignored
- Issues are managed without predetermined project controls
- The progress and status of the project is not monitored; rather, the budget and the time spent is monitored closely
- The project's controls are not set up properly and agreed upon

Each item on the list can be seen as a consequence of people not collaborating, not co-creating, and not pulling hard in the same direction to succeed with the project as an investment. Nothing is more important than the people involved, and they must come together and discuss, exchange ideas, viewpoints, and opinions, then make clear agreements.

The project's stakeholders must figure out how to succeed with the project – <u>together</u>.

3.2 System 1 vs System 2

According to Nobel Laureate Dr. Kahneman, people apply one of two systems when processing information and making decisions:

- System 1 is fast, effortless, intuitive, and emotional, often excluding people that are raising concerns and ignoring past performances.
- System 2 is slower, requires more effort, and is more logical. It is an inclusive and iterative decision process.

The People-focus mindset is about applying System 2. In fact, every element in best practice project management is about guiding people through the application of System 2 thinking and decision-making.

There are several powerful, mental shortcuts that can prevent people from making System 2 decisions:

- **Groupthink** is a psychological phenomenon in which independent critical thinking is replaced by consensus within a group. It is often on display in projects because of a basic facet of human nature people like to start projects more than not starting projects. Groupthink will push people into starting the project before it is ready, which often leads to hard crashes when foreseeable obstacles that should have been manageable get in the way.

- **Optimism Bias** is the tendency to overestimate the likelihood of positive events and underestimate the likelihood of negative events. Optimism bias can cause people to start projects that have a very high likelihood of failing, and projects that are not very good ideas to start with.
- **The Dunning-Kruger effect**, where people are unskilled and unaware of it. The Dunning-Kruger effect is a powerful mental bypass in which people believe that they are highly skilled in areas that they are unskilled in. Consequently, many people who have very low project management skills falsely believe that they are good at project management.
- **Lack of investment-focus and risk mindset** means that people are more prone to make fast decisions when deciding to start a project rather than being careful and prudent with the investment and the inherent risks.

The combined effect of Machine-focus, Project Triangle mindset, the lack of Investment-focus, and the above-mentioned cognitive biases results in a perfect størm of people who are prone to make poor investment decisions based on their current, incomplete understanding of the project as an investment, rather than performing due diligence and unearthing all of the key information that could inform more careful, prudent decision making.

Consequently, many projects begin with a System 1 decision that moves forward with unclear agreements and is thus started despite strong warning indicators that it would be more prudent not to start the project at the present time. People are generally prone to make System 1 decisions in projects but fail to understand that this is what is going on. To quote Kahneman:

"We can be blind to the obvious, and we are also blind to our blindness."

3.2.1 Overcoming System 1 decision making

It takes a huge effort and a good level of emotional restraint, especially at the beginning of a project, to overcome System 1 decision making, get rid of Machine-focus and the Project Triangle mindset, and replace these flawed mindsets with Investment-focus and People-focus.

To reduce or overcome System 1 decision making, people should collaborate, communicate, and co-create closely to create clear agreements on the eight project performance targets. This must be done via inclusive and iterative processes that allow people to analyze, understand, and own the project's consequences and clarify the change that the project should deliver. Experience has shown that this will not happen if the key stakeholders are merely reading the internal documents that are being distributed within the project. The key stakeholders have the most at stake. It is their project, and they must be deeply involved in making the agreements and decisions that will lead to a project's success.

Bruce Tuckman[10] developed a very useful, widely recognized model for how groups develop into highly effective collaborating teams. The model is based on four steps:

Forming - Størming - Norming – Performing

This happens at the project level when the project organization is appointed, and people move forward together to start, run, and close the project. The project organization will also loop through this process as people collaborate on getting things done, e.g.:

- When the project's Investment Case is discussed, and it is agreed to continue with the project
- When the project's requirements and scope are discussed and agreed upon
- During planning of the project and its stages
- Whenever a risk or issue is captured and analyzed, and appropriate actions are discussed and agreed upon

---

[10] Tuckman, B.W. *1965. Development Sequences in small Groups. Psychology Bulletin, 3(6), 384-99.*

Tuckman's model can explain why and how project management must be conducted via iterative, inclusive processes throughout the project to reduce or avoid System 1 decision making.

1. Forming in the project environment

The members of the project organization start by interacting around the task at hand, whether it is an Investment Case, the users' requirements, a plan, resolving a risk or an issue or sketching out one of the project's eight performance targets.

2. Størming in the project environment

As the members of the project team start discussing the task at hand, it is inevitable that conflicts, differing opinions, differing mindsets, and agendas will surface. This step may feel uncomfortable for some, while others may perceive this step as a waste of time, as they already have decided for themselves what the situation entails and how to best proceed. However, it is essential that the project team collaborate to apply rational, logical decision-making based on analysis and skills instead of rapid decision-making based on optimism bias and feelings.

Størming is often noisy and energetic but failing "to let the noise out of the project" via controlled størming processes will often lead to a very noisy, hostile project environment later in the project and increases the likelihood of the project starting to struggle and ultimately fail.

People need to be størming together, assessing each other's theories, ideas, and beliefs to reach joint agreements and a mutual understanding of the situation and of what must be done. This is what Dwight Eisenhower meant when he stated that *"plans are worthless, but planning is indispensable."* Communication and collaboration, størming and norming are all key to project success.

Consequently, people:

- need to take the time to communicate, to discuss, to align their perceptions, theories, ideas and understandings about the project and its objectives
- should embrace and welcome the chaos that often characterizes a project or decision in its infancy, since that chaos exists because people have not been størming and norming together.
- must be guided through the forming-størming-norming process, to agree upon/be shown the path to travel, the journey, and the goals

As a project manager, it is therefore important to understand that such noise and conflicts are an essential part of starting up the project and should therefore see it as a sign of two things; (1) the team is building a foundation for high-performance, and (2) vital information that increases the likelihood of the project being a good investment is being discovered.

3. Norming in the project environment

As the project team begins finding common ground and solutions together, the team begins communicating, collaborating, and co-creating as a team, centered around the necessary deliverables and tasks. At the start of the project, people begin to develop a common understanding of the project and the project's Investment Case, requirements, risk exposure, the path forward and what must be done to ensure that the project is a good investment and a good experience for all stakeholders.

4. Performing in the project environment

Once the team has collaborated to find common ground and solutions together, they can pull hard in the same direction to lead, manage, and control the project – to win with the project, together!

4 CHANGE IN AN ORGANIZATIONAL CONTEXT

Organizations often run projects, and it is therefore important to understand projects and change in an organization.

Organizations can be described simply as a simple system of business as usual (BAU) and changes to the BAU (Fig. 4.1). Overall, there are three types of changes to the BAU:

1) Implementing something **new** to the organization
2) **Improving something** that the organization is already doing
3) **Stop** doing something

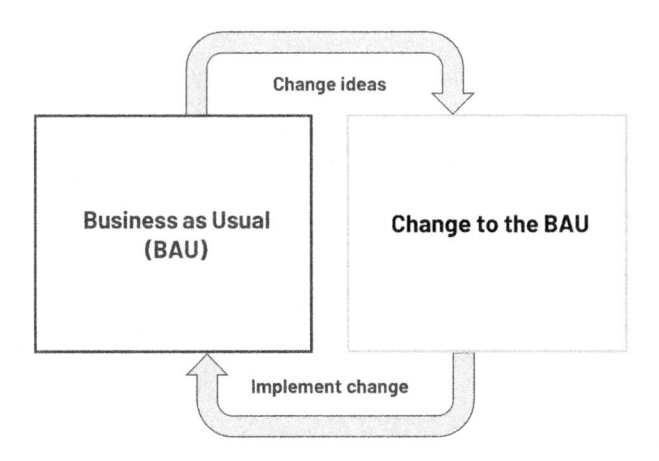

Fig. 4.1. An organization can be described as having two elements: business as usual (BAU) change to the BAU.

Change in an organization begins with the notion that something could, should, or must be changed. Internal or external issues, threats, or opportunities, whether perceived or real, trigger change ideas (Fig. 4.1). A change idea in its most basic form is an idea to change something in the organization, i.e., **to change the configuration of the organization, thereby making changes to the way it is running.**

The configuration of an organization is a snapshot of everything within an organization, e.g., its processes, products, services, people, skills, culture, governance, technology, inventory, infrastructure, governance structure, locations, reporting, quality and safety systems, logo, procurement processes, sales procedures, KPI's, OKR's and bonus set-up, strategic goals, mission and vision, and information management. In other words—*everything.*

In principle, every part of an organization's configuration carries the potential for change, so change ideas in an organization can be about anything. However, not all ideas are good, and what initially seems to be a brilliant idea may turn out to be the complete opposite. Sometimes, even ideas that are nearly certain to be beneficial should not be acted on immediately. Acting too quickly on a change idea can sometimes mean that focus and resources are leached away from the BAU and other, more desirable change ideas - never forget the dangers of System 1 thinking. Indeed, it is imperative that the people who can start an organizational change are aware of all consequences when they start a change initiative, and not just focus on the desired positive outcomes while ignoring the negative and potentially negative consequences.

4.1 Why have a strategy?

The purpose of an organization's strategy is to set the direction for the organization, to focus on and apply its resources to its strategic goals. Every organization has limits to its resources, and therefore cannot do everything, so the strategy should be geared towards helping the organization focus its investments so that the organization may achieve its overall purpose: to provide *value* to its owners in return for its resources. Every organization is owned. In the private sector, the owners are the shareholders, and in the public sector, the owners are the taxpayers. Therefore, the organization's strategy should play a central role in deciding which action should be taken with a change idea.

4.2 The three integrated elements in an organization

An organization therefore consists of three integrated elements: "business as usual" (BAU), the strategic layer, and the change portfolio (Fig. 4.2), respectively. Change ideas come from people in the BAU and at the strategic level. At the appropriate time, they are executed as projects as part of the organization's change portfolio.

Relatively slight changes to the configuration can simply be handed over to the BAU and put into use, whereas some changes require an active, well-planned implementation to create the Aspired new ways of working, while ensuring a stable BAU during and after the implementation of the change. A challenge is that it can be difficult to know up front whether a change is straightforward or complex before the uncertainties, pitfalls and all consequences have been analyzed – and owned!

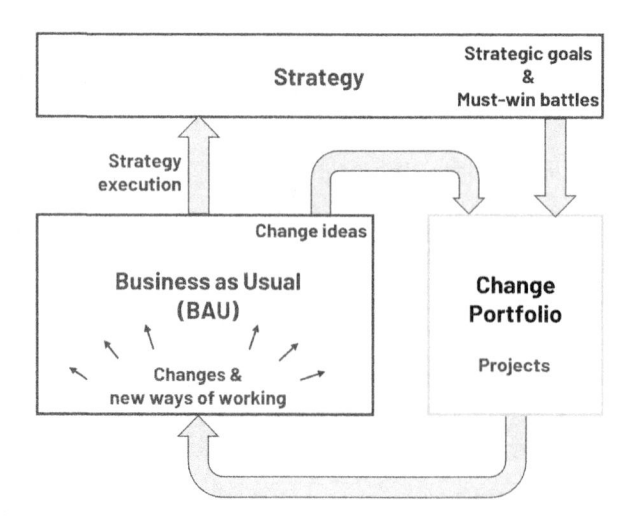

Fig. 4.2. Change in an organizational context.

4.3 What is a change portfolio?

A grouping of the organization's projects is called a change portfolio. An organization's change portfolio may be the totality of its change initiatives or, depending on the organization's structure, it may be arranged into several decentralized change portfolios.

Some organizations have formal portfolio management offices with well-defined processes and a governance structure. In other organizations, the change portfolio management is done informally, where people prioritize different change ideas on the go and manage the change initiatives on an ad hoc basis.

Whichever the change portfolio model is employed — centralized or decentralized, formally or informally managed, planned, or ad hoc portfolio management — an organization's change portfolio should consist of the set of change initiatives that can achieve the organization's strategy with the available resources. Consequently, the change ideas and change initiatives should be targeted towards the organization's strategic goals.

The connection between an organization's strategy and its projects is that:

Either the projects are contributing to successful strategy implementation, or it is drawing focus and resources away from more important projects.

Consequently, a key question when considering starting a project is:

Will the project actively contribute to achieving the organization's strategic goals, or not?

4.4 Everything can be changed

It is important to understand that, in principle, *everything in an organization can be changed!* This understanding should make it crystal clear regarding why people constantly produce new ideas to improve things, new ways of doing things smarter, faster, or better. However, this emphatically does not imply that *everything* should be changed. First, it would be unfathomably costly for an organization to constantly change everything in its configuration. Second, what would be the purpose? Not all ideas are good. Some ideas are even terrible, and not all good change ideas can be launched effectively, simply because organizations lack the resources to make all the changes that people in the organization desire. Furthermore, what at first seems like a fabulous change idea may not be so great once all its consequences are considered.

Consequently, the first element of change portfolio management is change portfolio prioritization and alignment, where change ideas are prioritized before they are stopped, put on hold, or implemented as change initiatives via change initiative management. If this element of change portfolio management is done correctly, the change portfolio of an organization should consist only of change initiatives that can execute the strategy. Therefore, the change portfolio of an organization should reveal the organization's strategy; that is, how the corporate management envisions the future path for the organization.

The second element of portfolio management is to ensure that the strategy is executed via successful projects, that is, to oversee and control the delivery of the pipeline of changes to the organization's configuration using project management.

5 A NEW MODEL FOR UNDERSTANDING PROJECTS

A commonly used term in project management is *"the project life cycle."* However, this is yet another common misunderstanding. A project cannot be described by a cycle. It may be argued that each stage or phase within a project follows a cycle, and then the next begins, like a spiral staircase leading to the ultimate goal. Also, a product can have a life cycle. However, a *project* cannot be described by a cycle. This is not about semantics: referring to a project as a cycle results in a severe misunderstanding, because it prevents people from understanding what projects really are, that is, the true nature of projects.

We uniquely describe a project as a value chain called the DIS/CREADIS Project Investment Chain®, which is a stepwise, change-creating, value-generating, strategy-executing progression from the start of the project to its conclusion (fig. 5.1).

The Project Investment Chain is universal, as it can be used to describe all projects and change initiatives. It can be used to track and explain the life of a change idea, from birth to sound investment. It provides a coherent, logical model of the entire system of deliverable management, quality management, project management, people change management, benefits management, and strategy execution, uniting the areas into one: Project Management.

The concept was first suggested by Trautner and Kolborg[11], but the current authors have since developed it into a powerful tool that can be used not only to explain the five management areas and their interconnectedness, but also to help set projects up to succeed, help people understand what project management is, and help them deal successfully with the central issues and confusion within project management.

The Project Investment Chain applies to all projects. Each project, and therefore each change, will have its own specific Project Investment Chain that tells a unique story about that project as an investment in change, and the individual links of the chain will be similarly well-defined. Before getting too excited about a change idea, the Project Investment Chain must be discussed, presented to stakeholders, and agreed-upon.

Each step in the Project Investment Chain is driven by the fact that a project is an investment in change. The change starts when someone has a notion that something could or should be changed in the organization, i.e., a **change idea**. This notion is triggered by a **problem, threat, or opportunity** caused by the old ways of working, or

---

[11] Andreas Trautner & Chris Kolborg. 2020. *The SIX – Why projects fail and how to succeed.*

operating, of the organization (OWoW). This is the root of projects, one end of the Project Investment Chain.

Implementing the change idea must bring the necessary **change** to the organization. Change can occur in two ways: Product changes in the form of a new, changed, or discontinued product/output/deliverable, and/or people change to create **new ways of working** for the organization that will deal with the problem, threat or opportunity caused by the organization's old ways of working, i.e., products – when people use the new or updated products – people change. Note here that product changes include both commercial products and/or services that bring about turnover to the organization, and all internal products not intended for commercial use (e.g., a new IT system).

This should **realize benefits** and **achieve strategic goals,** but these alone are insufficient to justify the project. To be truly successful, a project must also be a sound **investment**, which means that the positive consequences of the project must overshadow the negative consequences as detailed within the project parameters: Benefits, downsides, costs, time horizon and risks. As such, to be *a sound investment in change* the project's Investment Case must be scrutinized.

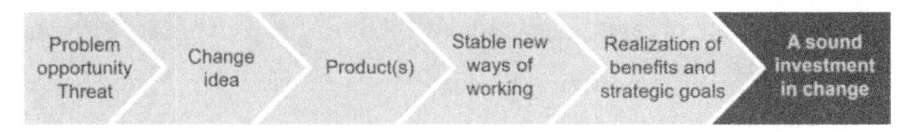

Fig. 5.1. The DIS/CREADIS Project Investment Chain®

It is important to stress that the change initiative value chain does not imply that change initiatives are unidirectional, stepwise progressions from left to right. Rather, it is a chain of elements where each element is carried out in iterations and is often re-visited.

What the Project Investment Chain does imply is that all elements must be considered, and all relevant elements in the Project Investment Chain must be managed, unless you spend your personal funds on the project! What you do with your own funds is entirely up to you.

However, the vast majority of people working on change initiatives are spending other people's funds and should therefore have to adhere to the rules of change initiative management and always maintain a strong focus on the full Project Investment Chain.

5.1 Important implications of the Project Investment Chain

The Project Investment Chain clarifies several vital properties of a project and project management:

1. A project is born with a change idea that is triggered by a problem, threat or an opportunity related to the current ways of working. To fully understand the change idea, it is imperative to understand the current ways of working and the problem, threat, or opportunity.

2. When project management is applied to a change idea, it becomes a project. If project management is not applied, it is just a change idea with people engaging in ad hoc activities.

3. Project management is about taking the change idea on a successful journey across the elements of the Project Investment Chain. The aim is to increase the likelihood of turning the change idea into a sound investment. Project management involves people being careful with the project investment and collaborating and co-creating to proactively manage and control potential risks and pitfalls that could prevent the project from becoming a sound investment.

4. It is via projects and therefore, project management that organizations make change happen successfully.

5. It is via projects and project management that organizations can successfully execute their strategy. Organizations that do not execute their projects successfully will not achieve their strategic goals and will find themselves unable execute their desired strategy. Project execution is therefore synonymous with strategy execution.

6. The Project Investment Chain reveals that a project is not necessarily successful even if benefits have been realized. The reason is that there

are parameters beyond benefits that must be satisfactorily met. A project is successful only if it is a sound investment, meaning that the positive consequences outweigh the negative consequences. Therefore, it follows that:

a) A project has failed if the negative consequences outweigh the positive consequences.
b) Even if the required products are delivered within a budget and deadline, and the people change is achieved, the project may still be a failure.
c) Even if a project delivered what was agreed upon, but exceeded the budget or the deadline, it may still be classified as successful, i.e., a successful investment.

An important implication of the Project Investment Chain is that projects are not restricted to changes that involve an organization. A project is simply *a change idea with something invested to make change happen and where one or more of the disciplines of project management are applied.* After all, the elements of best practice project management can be applied to a plethora of situations with huge benefits.

5.2 Uncertainties and pitfalls

Each element in the Project Investment Chain may be viewed as a risk category, where highly foreseeable (as well as emerging) risks and obstacles reduce the likelihood of the project becoming a successful investment in change. It requires a specific skill set to do so successfully, because the Project Investment Chain is shrouded in a cloud of uncertainties and pitfalls, some of which are listed in Table 1 below.

Table 1. Vital, universal uncertainties and pitfalls to the change initiative value chain.

1.	Is it clear which issues, threats, or opportunities we are targeting?
2.	Which specific, strategic goals will the change initiative help us achieve?
3.	What happens if we do not do the project?
4.	What options do we have to address the issues, threats, or opportunities?
5.	What change is needed to address the problem, threat, or opportunities?
6.	Are all the relevant stakeholders included?
7.	Is the change to new ways of working achievable and realistic?
8.	Can the organization run efficiently during and after the change?

9. What deliverables do we need to bring the required changes?

10. How will we approve the deliverables?

11. Who will approve the deliverables?

12. Who will be responsible for specifying the deliverables?

13. Who will create them?

14. Do we have negotiated robust agreements with the appropriate suppliers?

15. What value is expected from the change initiative?

16. What potentially adverse effects and downsides should we expect?

17. What threats and opportunities to the BAU will it bring?

18. Overall, how uncertain is the change initiative as an investment?

19. Do we have the necessary skills?

20. Do we have the necessary funds?

21. Do we have the necessary time?

22. How good are we at running projects in general?

23. *How and when do we measure whether the change initiative was a sound investment?*

24. *How and when will we measure the strategic contribution?*

25. *Who will be accountable for the strategic contribution?*

26. *Who will be accountable for the investment, the ROI, and the negative consequences?*

27. *Overall, is this an effective way for us to spend the owner's funds?*

28. *Are there better ways for us to spend the owner's funds?*

29. *Who will be concerned about the team's well-being?*

30. *What will we do, in what order and when?*

31. *How do we manage emerging problems, changes, and uncertainties?*

The good news is that the uncertainties and pitfalls shrouding the Project Investment Chain are highly foreseeable and well-known, and they can be managed and controlled proactively with best practice project management before they become problems or explode into crisis.

5.3 The stakeholders and the psychological contract

When considering launching a change initiative, all elements of the Project Investment Chain must be considered, and all uncertainties and pitfalls shrouding the value chain should be managed proactively to avoid or reduce the likelihood of them becoming insurmountable obstacles.

This requires the right mindsets and strong project management skills. Without this, the likelihood of uncertainties becoming big problems and morphing into full-blown crises is relatively high. This is therefore an essential discussion that the stakeholders must have from the start of the project:

How can we make the change idea into a sound investment in change?

Hereunder, to discuss with the stakeholders: *How are we going to control the project, how uncertain is the investment and what can we do to increase the likelihood of succeeding with the project?*

You can skip these discussions only if you are spending your own funds on the project, or if you have a clear, predetermined agreement with the investors. It is only in these limited cases that you can choose *not* to be mindful of the Project Investment Chain and not to apply project management. The likelihood of failing will be relatively high, but it may be that you have some risk-willing capital to invest, and what you do with your own funds is entirely up to you.

However, most people working on change initiatives are spending other people's funds and resources, and in most cases, they want something in return. Therefore, a project is based on a psychological contract: *All involved must do whatever they can to make the project a sound investment, and if that is not possible, to do everything to ensure that the project will not be a horrific investment.* This requires mindsets and skills, as well as people adhering to the rules of project management, maintaining a strong focus on the full change initiative value chain, and to approach everything with an abundance of carefulness and prudence. People must be mindful of not jeopardizing the organization's brand and reputation, the customer relationship, the supplier relationship, and the team's well-being and of the owners' funds.

6 CONCLUSIONS

We set out on a long journey to understand why projects fail and why so many projects fail. We now understand exactly why.

When people review failed projects, these are the reasons that are typically attributed to project failure:

- The project's Business Case is poorly understood
- Scope creep
- The required features and functionalities are unclear and not agreed-upon
- Unclear roles and responsibilities
- Poor planning
- Lack of quality planning and quality control
- The element of people change is ignored or poorly managed
- Poor risk management, i.e., ignoring or accepting huge risks
- Lack of control of the project's progress and status
- Biases, heuristics, and mental shortcuts are preventing people from starting and running successful projects

However, these are merely *reasons* for project failure. As dictated by the area of risk management, we must always search for the *root cause*; the powerful, systemic error that not only prevents people from starting and managing their projects well, but also from improving their project culture. Arguably, when people report these reasons for project failure, they demonstrate a very serious flaw in their understanding of risk and issue management.

We have indeed identified an immensely powerful root cause. It is so simple and so obvious, yet it took a while to understand its titanic implications: people misunderstand what a project is, its purpose and what it means to succeed or fail with a project. So naturally, they simply misunderstand what project management is, as well as what project success and failure is.

People usually believe that a project is about delivering something within a deadline and a budget, so most projects are started with this focus. Unfortunately, it means that most projects are started with a strong focus on the wrong parameters. We call this *"the Project Triangle Mindset."* A consequence of this flawed mindset is that people cannot apply the best practice elements effectively and furthermore, they misunderstand what project management is all about.

So why is this so important? Imagine a team of football players that fail to understand what football is about, and how to win or lose a game? Or picture two chess-players playing a game of chess, but one player is misunderstanding what the game is about and how the chess-pieces can move?

The combined effect of people misunderstanding the mindset and lacking the project management skills is titanic: Not only are many people not able to start and run a project as an investment, but the lack of project management skills prevents them from even managing the project with focus on producing, reviewing, and approving the required deliverables. Just doing that part of a project successfully requires strong skills in quality management, planning, risk management, issue management as well as being able to report on the progress against the plan.

However, because the project triangle is often applied with the biggest focus on time and cost, these essential skills are rarely applied well because they are overruled by *"the need for speed"* to keep the costs low.

6.1 A short and simple truth about projects

As we have discussed, project management is built upon on a simple, logical, and undeniable truth:

A project is an investment in change.

Furthermore, and this is essential: It is an investment in change that is *made by people, for people*. This is the first element of the project fundamentals (fig. 6.1). When people fully comprehend and own this undeniable and logical truth, it provides them with two patterns of thinking, mindsets, or paradigms: Investment-focus and People-focus. The two mindsets can be seen as logical consequences of the logical truth of projects, and they will guide and govern people's every decision and all actions in a project. Together, they inform the Project Investment Chain®, which illustrates the value-creating, strategy-executing steps that can describe all projects.

```
Problem          Change                    Stable new    Realization      A sound
Opportunity      idea      Product(s)      ways of       of benefits      investment
Threat                                     working       and strategic    in change
                                                         goals
```

The Project Investment Chain

Mindsets

Investment-focus   People-focus

A project is an Investment in change

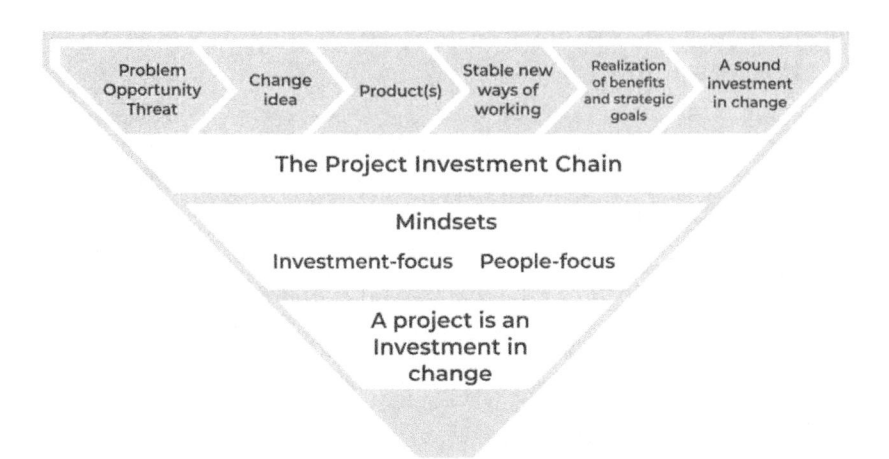

Fig. 6.1. The project fundamentals are based on the logical truth of what a project is – and provide a solid foundation for the best practice project management elements.

The project fundamentals provide a new, clear paradigm and a new model that can help people and organizations cope with the challenges that arise within the area of project management, change and strategy execution. As such, it provides a foundation for project management; mindsets that are cardinal for effective application of best practice project management skills. It also provides us with four clear definitions and insights:

1) A successful project means that the project is a sound investment in change for the key stakeholders
2) A project has failed if it is not a sound investment in change for the key stakeholders
3) Project management is the craft of doing everything possible to ensure that a project will become a sound investment in change, and if that is not possible; to prevent the project from becoming a horrific investment in change. It is done by managing uncertainties and obstacles that the change idea may encounter on its journey across the Project Investment Chain, hereunder:
   a. Well-known, generic risks
   b. Emerging risks
   c. Risk that materializes into issues
4) Projects fail because uncertainties and obstacles are ignored or otherwise poorly managed; most of which are known, highly foreseeable and manageable. However, people often fail to focus on the full set of project variables of the investment in change. In essence, projects fail because they are set up to fail from the very start because people are not being mindful of the

investment, and therefore fail to apply the powerful elements of best practice project management, hereunder:

a. Clarifying the Project's Investment Chain
b. Revealing and agreeing upon the project's true investment case
c. Setting up a dedicated project organization headed by the Project Owner
d. Capturing and agreeing upon the requirements of the change
e. Planning the change
f. Managing risk and issues
g. Monitoring progress and status

6.2 The Project Investment Chain® by DIS/CREADIS

In this book, we presented a coherent, logical model of the entire system of deliverable management, quality management, project management, people change management, benefits management, and strategy execution, uniting the five areas into one: Project Management. This representation of a project will help people and organizations set up their projects to succeed from the start and manage their projects successfully throughout the life of the project to become a sound investment in change.

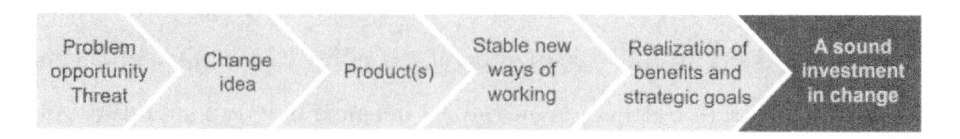

| Problem opportunity Threat | Change idea | Product(s) | Stable new ways of working | Realization of benefits and strategic goals | A sound investment in change |

Fig. 6.2. The DIS/CREADIS Project Investment Chain®

6.3 We already have what it takes

An important implication of the Project Investment Chain is that whenever you want to achieve a change – then you can consider it a project. Why is this important? Well, because we know how to get projects to succeed: by the skillful application of best practice project management. Best practice project management has been developed over the last five decades for this very purpose: to manage uncertainties and obstacles that can challenge or even derail a project completely. Hence, we have a complete set of methods we can use to ensure the sound investment of the project. Risk-, quality-, and issue management, the Investment Case, Planning, monitoring, and controlling the progress and status, the project organization, and elements like people change management and benefits management. If you want to achieve a change, you can benefit from applying these elements *as long as you are mindful of tailoring them to the situation.*

The best practice project management elements are not exclusive for big projects – they are a part of life where system 2 decisions are beneficial.

It is therefore imperative that we internalize the fact that the essence of project management is to ensure that the change idea can traverse the Investment Chain successfully by coping with the uncertainties and issues that lurk along the project investment chain. Without proper and effective project management, a project has a high likelihood of failing

– and that is exactly why most projects in organizations fail, as stated by the PRINCE2 manual. If you just embark on a change journey while ignoring the common and well-known risks and obstacles and not applying project management to deal with them, you will most likely fail. Ignoring risks is therefore not a recommended risk response. Nevertheless, this is what many people and organizations do on a daily basis.

As such, project management is not a guarantee that a project will succeed. However, it can dramatically increase the likelihood of the project becoming a successful investment in change, and this is important because as can be seen from the Project Investment Chain, the humble project holds a mighty punch: projects and project management are how organizations can deliver their strategic goals successfully! No more and certainly no less. An organization that is not applying proper project management will fail with most of its projects – and it will therefore fail to implement its strategy. This is exactly why so many organizational strategies fail and must be "re-vitalized" and re-visited in the next corporate strategy.

Indeed, the organizational landscape is littered with struggling, failing, and failed projects – and strategies. But we already have what it takes – IF we understand the foundation for all projects and change initiatives:

- A project is an investment in change
- Project management is investment in change-management
- A Project Manager is an investment in change-manager
- A Project Owner is an investment in change owner
- All projects must traverse The Project Investment Chain to be successful
- Project management is about taking the change idea on a successful journey across the entire Project Investment Chain – or making sure that the idea is stopped before being launched as a project
- Project management requires two mindsets: Investment-focus and People-focus
- Project management also requires people highly skilled in the craft of project management

7 PERSPECTIVATION

It is important to understand that we have not developed a new way to manage projects. There is simply no need for this. The solution for running successful change initiatives has been around for decades; it is called "best practice project management." We can clearly see that whenever we apply best practice project management correctly to a project, we achieve remarkable results.

However, a precondition for applying it correctly is that the application of the elements of best practice project management is based on the project fundamentals, hereunder the two mindsets and the Project's Investment Chain *that are dictated by the logical truth of what a project is*.

7.1 Discovering what was hidden

It is also important to stress that as such, we did not invent the project fundamentals. As archaeologists, we simply discovered what was always there, but hidden - the logical truth about projects and, therefore, project management.

Armed with our newfound knowledge, we went to work to reduce the complexity of such a daunting process by defining and describing the terms, developing, structuring, and conceptualizing them into an explicit representation that has always contained the project fundamentals that project management must be based upon, even though many of us have spent our careers in, and sometimes out of, the swamp.

If you study the best of the best practice methodologies as closely as we did and know what to look for, you will detect both the blurred outlines of the mindsets as well as faint hints of the Project Investment Chain. They are embedded implicitly within the methodologies because best practice project management is not only based upon them – it simply cannot be executed without them.

For the relatively few people that already skillfully apply the project fundamentals when they start and manage projects, this book will bring clarity to the way they speak the language of project management. Make no mistake, project management *is* a language. It consists of words that have specific meanings, like business case, planning, project owner, risk management, lessons learned. These words, or concepts, get their true and accurate meaning from the project fundamentals.

Hereof follows that if you do not understand the project fundamentals or misunderstand them as many do and instead apply the Project Triangle mindset and Machine-focus, you will not understand the terms. For example, you will never be able to fully understand what a business case is, or what a project owner is. You will therefore fail to understand and speak the language of project management. This is, in a nutshell, why so many projects fail. We are back at the ancient tale of the Tower of Babylon and the words of Socrates:

"The beginning of wisdom is the definition of terms."

For a large group of people that have misunderstood the project fundamentals and therefore have been unable to understand or speak the language of project management, comprehending what is in this book will dramatically and fundamentally change the elemental meanings that lie in the vocabulary of project management.

Like learning any language, this will take time and require an effort, but doing so will enable people and organizations to consistently start and manage successful projects. Indeed, one of our primary motivations for authoring this book is to bring the differing dialects of project management closer together, to ensure that all involved share a similar understanding of the terms and methodologies employed by project management.

There is much at stake. To quote from the famous and wonderful paper by Kruger and Dunning[12]:

"The skills that enable one to construct a grammatical sentence are the same skills necessary to recognize a grammatical sentence, and thus

---

[12] Justin Kruger & David Dunning. 2009. *Unskilled and Unaware of It: How Difficulties in Recognizing One's Own Incompetence Lead to Inflated Self-Assessments*. Psychology, 2009, 1, 30-46

are the same skills necessary to determine if a grammatical mistake has been made. In short, the same knowledge that underlies the ability to produce correct judgment is also the knowledge that underlies the ability to recognize correct judgment. To lack the former is to be deficient in the latter."

Therefore, this book is aimed at changing the status quo and steering project management on a more sustainable course, where our (global) resources are spent on projects that will bring real, tangible, and true value creation. Best practice project management is exactly what the words describe – best practice. But we currently lack an established, commonly-held mindset that will lead us to an agreed-upon understanding of *why* we do projects and *what* projects should bring about, and we also lack an established, commonly-held mindset of *how* we must do project management. As such, if practitioners and academia can unite under the banner of the simple and logical truths revealed in this book, we can start to reap the full benefits of these best practices.

7.2 A note on sustainability

Sustainability is a hot topic and therefore top-of-mind – luckily. However, there is a different kind of sustainability in the realm of project management – project sustainability. It is both its own domain, but also something that, in very real ways, affects the conventional domain of sustainability. For instance, if we know that roughly 50-75 % of all projects globally are struggling or even failing – well, then we are wasting an enormous number of resources that could have been spent on transforming our world into a more sustainable place. Furthermore, all these struggling and failing projects are not very sustainable for human beings. Due to this, we believe it to be a key player in the number of human beings diagnosed with stress or other illnesses. Remember, projects are conducted *by people*, which means that individuals are always involved and therefore, at risk of being harmed by a capsizing project. If we can succeed in starting the *right* projects, turning down the poor investment cases and managing our projects as investments, we will greatly improve our chances of directing more resources to other purposeful matters, while taking diligent care of our employees, colleagues, and stakeholders.

7.3 Concluding words

For anyone involved in projects, this book is must-read. For someone who is accountable for executing successful projects and turning strategies into results, this book is of the essence because the realization of your strategic goals goes through successful projects. Organizations need to be able to start the right projects and to manage them with great skills – and the right mindsets.

In today's fast-paced world where the focus is unfortunately often on quick results, the mindset that people apply when starting projects is often a "let's do something now"- mentality. As a result, many expensive, well-intentioned strategies have failed during execution.

Money, time, and initiative that should have helped the organization win in the market are too often poured down the drain due to poor project management practices.

Basing your strategy execution on a weak project management culture is like building castles on a swamp. The strong point made in this book is that people and organizations must reset and rethink the way they do projects. That journey starts by applying the strong, rigorous foundation we call "The Project Fundamentals" and with that, the brilliant DIS/CREADIS Project Investment Chain, which is a groundbreaking, systematic approach to projects. Because it will help you start the right projects, manage them well and successfully execute your strategy.

With this book, we have shown you a fresh path for project management and hopefully, encouraged you to walk it. What is in this book is definitely worth investing the time to internalize and master but that is a path that you must decide to walk – with strong commitment - if you want to become a craftsman or -woman within project management.

Andreas and Lasse

Denmark, December 2024

Printed in Great Britain
by Amazon